broken thirds

(one string)

for the cello

book two

by cassia harvey

CHP310
©2018 C. Harvey Publications All Rights Reserved.
www.charveypublications.com - print books
www.learnstrings.com - PDF downloadable books
www.harveystringarrangements.com - chamber music

Broken Thirds (One String) for the Cello, Book Two

2

Broken Thirds (One String) for the Cello, Book Two

Broken Thirds (One String) for the Cello, Book Two

4

Broken Thirds (One String) for the Cello, Book Two

©2018 C. Harvey Publications All Rights Reserved.

5

Broken Thirds (One String) for the Cello, Book Two

Broken Thirds (One String) for the Cello, Book Two

©2018 C. Harvey Publications All Rights Reserved.

6

Broken Thirds (One String) for the Cello, Book Two

7

Broken Thirds (One String) for the Cello, Book Two

8

Broken Thirds (One String) for the Cello, Book Two

9

This entire page is played on the D string.

Broken Thirds (One String) for the Cello, Book Two   **This entire page is played on the D string**

Broken Thirds (One String) for the Cello, Book Two

10

This entire page is played on the D string.

©2018 C. Harvey Publications All Rights Reserved.

Broken Thirds (One String) for the Cello, Book Two
This entire page is played on the D string.

This entire page is played on the D string.

11

Broken Thirds (One String) for the Cello, Book Two

©2018 C. Harvey Publications All Rights Reserved.

24

12

Broken Thirds (One String) for the Cello, Book Two

This entire page is played on the D string.

Slow, with vibrato

©2018 C. Harvey Publications All Rights Reserved.

Broken Thirds (One String) for the Cello, Book Two   **This entire page is played on the D string**

13

This entire page is played on the D string.

Broken Thirds (One String) for the Cello, Book Two
This entire page is played on the D string. 27

©2018 C. Harvey Publications All Rights Reserved.

14

This entire page is played on the D string.

Broken Thirds (One String) for the Cello, Book Two — This entire page is played on the D string

Broken Thirds (One String) for the Cello, Book Two — This entire page is played on the D string.

Broken Thirds (One String) for the Cello, Book Two   This entire page is played on the D string. 33

©2018 C. Harvey Publications All Rights Reserved.

Also available from www.charveypublications.com: CHP349
The Saint-Saëns Cello Concerto No. 1 Study Book, Vol. 1

Concerto
Section One: Measures 1-7

Concerto, by Camille Saint-Saëns
Exercises by Cassia Harvey

Learning the Notes and the First Shift
Measures 1, 5

©2019 C. Harvey Publications All Rights Reserved.

www.ingramcontent.com/pod-product-compliance
Lightning Source LLC
Chambersburg PA
CBHW051428070526
44584CB00023B/3632